A New True Book

THE ARCTIC

By Lynn M. Stone

CHILDRENS PRESS™

CHICAGO

Airplane landing at Frosbisher in the Arctic

PHOTO CREDITS

Steve McCutcheon—Cover, 29, 42 (right), 44 (2 photos)

Valan Photos:
© Denis Roy—41 (right), 42 (left), 43
© Don Loveridge—2
© Pam Hickman—17
© Steve Krasemann—24 (2 photos), 33 (left)
© Wayne Lankinen—26 (right), 30 (left), 33 (right)
© Brian Milne—10 (left)

Tom Stack & Associates:
© B. Crader—41 (left)
© Rod Allin—4 (top), 19 (right), 23 (left), 30 (right)
© Dale Johnson—22, 45
© Mark Newman—25
© Tom Stack—34 (right)

Lynn M. Stone—6, 10 (right), 12 (2 photos), 14, 15 (2 photos), 19 (left), 20, 23 (right), 26 (left), 27 (2 photos), 31 (2 photos), 34 (left), 35, 36 (2 photos), 38 (2 photos), 39 (2 photos)

American Petroleum Institute—8

Len Meents—4 (bottom)

Cover: Flocks of ptarmigan gather during the Arctic winter

Library of Congress Cataloging in Publication Data

Stone, Lynn M.
  The arctic.

  (A New true book)
  Includes index.
  Summary: Describes the Arctic, including its seasons, geographical features, animal life, and people.
    1.   Natural history—Arctic Regions—Juvenile literature.   2.   Arctic Regions—Juvenile literature. [1.   Arctic Regions]   I.   Title.
  QH84.1.S76   1985   508.3'113   84-23248
  ISBN 0-516-01935-X   AACR2

TABLE OF CONTENTS

Baby polar bear

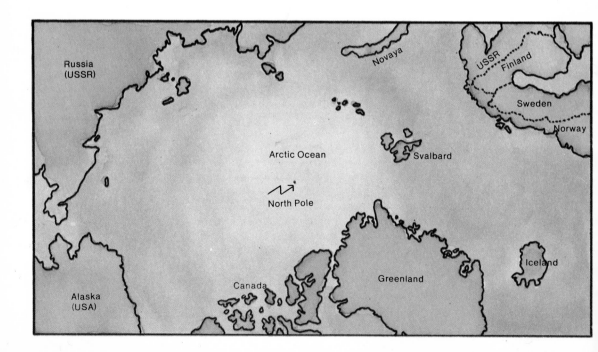

THE ARCTIC

The Arctic is the land and sea at the top of the world. It is a huge area that touches seven countries: Canada, the United States, Greenland, Iceland, Russia, Norway, and Finland.

The Arctic is often called the Land of Midnight Sun.

Midnight in the Arctic summer

During the Arctic summer
the sun never sets. Then
the Arctic is never
completely dark, even at
midnight. But there are
days in winter when the
sun never rises!

ARCTIC SEASONS

The Arctic is one of the coldest places on earth. Winter temperatures reach minus 70 degrees Fahrenheit. For months the temperatures are below zero. Parts of the Arctic are always covered by ice.

The Arctic winter lasts nearly eight months. Much of the land is white with snow. The ocean is frozen.

The ground is frozen. The
wind blows. Most of the
animals have left. Many of
those that remain are
hidden in snow tunnels.

The Arctic spring begins with longer days of sunlight. Snow slowly melts. River ice cracks and moves in blocks. The upper few inches of ground thaw.

By June much of the Arctic land is free from snow. Thousands of birds arrive from the south. Plants begin to grow. Insects appear. Herds of caribou move northward.

Arctic poppy (left) and dwarf rhododendron (right)

Days of endless sunlight begin. Temperatures reach 70 degrees Fahrenheit.

But summer is brief. Shorter days and colder nights begin. Snow flurries fall. Animals leave. Ice forms. Autumn arrives.

FOREST-TUNDRA

To reach the Arctic you
must travel north through
great evergreen forests. As
you travel farther north the
trees become scattered
and smaller.

In summer the ground
here is wet and soft. Much
of it is covered by grasses.
Some of the ground is
hidden under a light,

Caribou moss (left)
and stunted trees (right)
grow on the Arctic tundra.

spongy plant called caribou moss. This type of northern land is called forest-tundra.

The last tall evergreens grow in the forest-tundra.

ARCTIC TUNDRA

North of the forest-tundra, trees do not grow tall. The soil is too thin and there is ice in the ground. Also, it is cold and windy much of the year.

This open, grassy land is the true Arctic tundra. It is a grassland; sometimes it is called "Arctic prairie." Much of the tundra is under a blanket of small

Tundra

plants that grow close to
the ground. A few grow in
cracks between rocks.

Tundra plants grow very
slowly. Even tiny plants
may be several years old.
Plants with flowers grow
alongside moss and

Lichens (left) on rocks and dwarf
birch trees (right) are tundra plants.

lichens. Lichens can be
soft like sponges or rough
like tree bark. Lichens do
not have flowers, but they
are colorful.

The land seems treeless.
But willow and birch trees
just a few inches tall grow
on the tundra.

15

Tundra covers much of the Arctic region. Very little rain falls in the Arctic. In fact, the Arctic gets about as much rain as a desert!

In summer tundra ponds are everywhere. Because only a few inches of tundra ground ever thaws, the melting snow cannot soak into the ground. Ice stops water from draining deeper. The water collects in ponds and lakes.

The most northern Arctic
lands are very cold and
dry. The land rises in
many mountains and
strange shapes. Some of it
is always covered by ice.
Very few plants and
animals can live here.

THE ARCTIC OCEAN

The Arctic lands surround the Arctic Ocean. The ocean has salt water, and salt water usually doesn't freeze. But the Arctic Ocean is so cold that it freezes from shore to shore in winter! Warmer weather melts some of the ice and keeps parts of the ocean open.

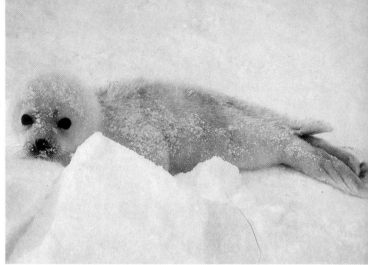

Walrus (left) and seals live in the Arctic.
When the baby harp seal (above) grows up, its
fur will be brown.

Although it is very cold,
the Arctic Ocean has a
variety of plants and
animals. Tiny ocean plants
use sunlight to grow. The
plants are eaten by fish
and little hard-shelled
animals. They, in turn, are
eaten by seals, walrus, and

seabirds. Seals are food for polar bears.

Giant whales swim into open patches of the Arctic Ocean. They eat the tiny plants and animals.

Humpback whale

ANIMALS OF THE TUNDRA

People sometimes think the Arctic is barren, or without life. A large area of Canada's tundra is even called "the barren grounds."

In fact, the summer tundra is full of life! The plants that color it are food for the Arctic animals. Without the summer plants, there would be no animals.

The mouse-like lemming eats tundra plants. It is

Lemmings live in the Arctic.

one of the few animals
that lives in the Arctic all
year long. In winter
lemmings live in tunnels
under the snow. The snow
keeps the cold Arctic air
from the lemmings.

The Arctic hare is a
large rabbit. It eats plants.
Its feet, like the lemming's,

Arctic hare (left) and
Arctic ground squirrel (above)

are very furry. The fur
helps the hare hop across
the snow.

The Arctic ground
squirrel is a plant eater,
too. When winter comes, it
goes into a long, deep
sleep in its burrow.

The biggest Arctic plant
eaters are the musk ox

Musk ox

and caribou. The musk ox
lives on the far northern
tundra. A musk ox can
weigh eight hundred
pounds.

Caribou live in great
herds that travel long
distances. They eat moss

Male caribou are called bulls.

and lichens. When winter approaches, most caribou travel south into forests.

In Europe and Asia, caribou are called reindeer. Their skin is used for clothing. They also can be used for milk and meat. Reindeer are raised by farmers like sheep.

In summer the short-tailed weasel
has a brown coat (left). In winter
its coat will be white (right).

The animals that eat
plants often become food
for meat-eating animals.

The short-tailed weasel
is the smallest of the
meat-eating hunters. In
summer it is brownish, like

The Arctic fox also changes to a white coat in winter.

the tundra. In winter it
turns white to match the
snow. The weasel's ability
to change its color is
called camouflage.

The Arctic fox is gray
and brown in the summer.

It turns white in the winter. Its thick, white, winter coat is very valuable.

The Arctic fox is a hunter, but it will also eat meat left behind by other animals. Sometimes a fox follows a polar bear. When the bear leaves part of its meal, the fox finishes it.

The polar bear is the most powerful meat eater in the Arctic. It can weigh one thousand pounds!

The polar bear walks and swims long distances.

It lives for several months on the Arctic ice. The bear hunts seals by waiting at holes that seals keep open in the ice. When a seal pops up, the bear kills it.

29

Mother polar bear and her cubs (left) and Arctic wolf (right)

In summer polar bears come ashore. The females look for dens and have their babies. They eat berries, mushrooms, and even garbage when they are on land.

The wolf is another powerful Arctic hunter. On the tundra it eats mostly small animals, but groups of wolves can kill caribou and musk ox.

Almost one hundred kinds of birds nest on the tundra each summer. The tundra has plenty of insects and plants, the food most birds eat.

Nest of an Arctic tern (left) and snow goose goslings (below)

Most birds arrive as the snow melts. Nest building begins at once. Since there are no tall trees, the birds nest on the ground or on cliffs.

Nests on the ground look like tundra plants. The birds themselves are usually brown, so they are hard to see, too.

When the first snow falls, most birds fly south. They would not be able to find food during an Arctic winter.

Willow ptarmigan (above) nests on the ground. Its feathers become white in winter (right).

The ptarmigan, however, stays on the tundra. The ptarmigan is brown in summer. In the winter, it turns white, just as the weasel and fox do.

The snowy owl usually spends the entire year in the Arctic. Snowy owls live mostly on lemmings.

Golden plover (above) and snowy owl (right)

Lemmings are hard to find in some years. Then the owl has to fly south to hunt.

Shorebirds nest in the Arctic. Their eggs are colored like the tundra itself. The golden plover is one of the most beautiful

Arctic tern

and best-known shorebirds. In autumn the golden plover flies to South America.

When the Arctic tern leaves the north, it flies south all the way to Antarctica! Its trip is the longest of any bird in the world.

Nesting eider duck (left) and an old-squaw (right)

Ducks build nests of down. Mother ducks pluck these soft feathers from their breasts.

The down of eider ducks is sometimes used for clothing, pillows, and blankets. It is very warm.

A pretty brown and white

duck also nests on the tundra. This duck's loud call sounds like an old Indian woman. The duck is called the old-squaw.

Thousands of swans and snow geese nest in the Arctic. Most of them are as white as Arctic snow. Some are dark.

The snow geese, and most other Arctic geese, nest in groups called colonies. Adult geese join together to chase hunting

A snow goose (left) flaps its wings to drive hunting animals away from its nest. Herring gulls (right) will eat the eggs of other birds.

animals away from their nests.

Gulls and jaegers will eat the eggs of other birds. Snow geese always watch out for these hunters.

The tallest bird of the Arctic is the sandhill crane.

Jaeger (left) and sandhill crane (right) are hunters.

(Swans are the heaviest birds.) The crane stands almost as tall as a human. The cranes nest by themselves. They eat insects and other small animals. They will even eat baby geese and lemmings.

PEOPLE IN THE ARCTIC

People have lived in the Arctic for thousands of years. Many of these people are known as Eskimo. But they call themselves Inuit, which means "human beings."

Arctic people hunted with spears, lines, and knives. They ate the animal meat. They used skins and fur for clothing. They hunted whales, seals, walrus, polar

The Inuit have lived in the Arctic regions of Canada and Alaska for thousands of years.

bears, caribou, and foxes. They learned to live with cold and hunger. They learned to build snow houses called igloos.

The igloo (above) is a symbol of the Inuit's past. The Alaskan pipeline is one symbol of their future.

The ways of Arctic people changed after outsiders came.

The outsiders' ways were not always good for the Arctic people. Many Inuit died from diseases brought by visitors.

Today Arctic people do

In an Inuit village today, the houses are built of wood.

not need to hunt and make their clothes from skins. They can buy their food and clothes at stores. They hunt with rifles. They still have dogs and sleds, but they also have snowmobiles.

Snowmobiles are used to travel in the Arctic today, but the Inuit still use dog sleds.

The Arctic people have changed and so has the Arctic itself. Oil and minerals have been discovered. More and more people visit the Arctic. Fewer caribou live on the tundra.

Most of the Arctic is still clean and wild. But the

Arctic can be spoiled
easily. Damage does not
heal quickly—if at all—in
the cold Arctic. People
must protect the Arctic.
Then it will remain one of
the earth's greatest treasures.

WORDS YOU SHOULD KNOW

ability(uh • BILL • it • ee)—being able to do something

barren(BEAR • un)—empty; not covered with plants or trees

burrow(BURR • oh)—a hole or tunnel made in the ground by an animal

camouflage(KAM • uh • flaj)—the ability to hide by changing colors or using some other way to hide

cliff(KLIF)—a high, steep face of rock, earth, or other natural material rising up from the ground

den(DEN)—a cave or a hollow used by a wild animal for hiding or sleeping

down(DOWN)—very soft and fluffy feathers, usually from the breast of a duck or goose

Fahrenheit(FAIR • en • hite)—the thermometer scale of reading temperatures on which freezing is 32 degrees and boiling point of water is 212 degrees above zero

flurries(FLER • eez)—a very light snowfall

forest-tundra(FOR • est—TUN • drah)—the place between a forest and tundra, usually with few large trees scattered over soggy ground that is covered with grasses and other plants

grassland(GRASS • land)—land covered by types of grass

herd(HERD)—a large group of animals that keeps together

igloo(IG • loo)—a house made by Eskimo people out of blocks of snow

lichens(LIE • kinz)—small plants able to grow on a solid surface, as rock

moss(MAWSS)—a class of plants, usually growing in wet or damp areas, that have tiny stems or leaves

prairie(PRAIR • ee)—a large grassland on which grow many types of grasses and few trees

shorebirds(SHOAR • burds)—birds that live along the shore of an ocean or sea

thaw(THAW) — melt; to go from being frozen to being liquid
tundra(TUN • drah) — cold place with permanantly frozen subsoil on which grow only tiny trees and plants
valuable(VAL • yoo • ah • bil) — having value; worth a good deal of money

INDEX

About the Author

Lynn M. Stone was born and raised in Meriden, Connecticut. He received his undergraduate degree from Aurora College in Illinois and his master's degree from Northern Illinois University. Once a teacher in Sarasota, Florida, Mr. Stone currently teaches English to junior high school students in the West Aurora Public School system.

A free-lance wildlife photographer and journalist, Lynn has had his work appear in many publications including National Wildlife, Ranger Rick, Oceans, Country Gentleman, Animal Kingdom, *and* International Wildlife. *He has also contributed to* Time-Life. National Geographic, Audubon Field Guide, *and Hallmark Cards publications.*

Many of Lynn Stone's photographs have been used in the New True Books published by Childrens Press.